Philippians

At His Feet Studies

By Hope A. Blanton and Christine B. Gordon

19Baskets

Philippians: At His Feet Studies
© 2018 by Hope A. Blanton and Christine B. Gordon
ISBN 978-1-946862-02-0

19Baskets, Inc.
PO Box 31291
Omaha, NE 68131
https://19baskets.com

First Edition

Cover design by Sophie Calhoun

Photography by Rebecca Tredway

At His Feet Story

A few years ago, Hope started looking for materials for the women's fall Bible study at our church. While she found a great number of quality Bible studies, she had a hard time finding studies written for women by women who were reformed. She also had a tough time finding in depth studies of the scripture that didn't take a whole lot of time. In a moment of desperation, Hope asked Chris if she would be willing to co-write a study on Romans, convincing her by asking, "I mean, really, how hard could it be?" And so it began. Weekly emails back and forth, Chris deep in commentaries, Hope mulling over questions, tweaking, editing, asking, pondering. A group of women at Redeemer Presbyterian Church in Lincoln, Nebraska patiently bore with us as we experimented with them every week, and learned to find our rhythm as writers.

Two years later, Hope approached Chris again, softening her up by telling her she could choose any book she wanted. I Samuel it was. Old Testament narrative is the best. Another study was born. About this time, women started asking us for copies of the two studies we had written. While trying to send endless pdfs to people around the country via email, a pastor friend who happens to be a publisher approached Chris and Hope at a party, offering to publish their Bible studies. Suddenly, they had a way to get these into the hands of women who could use them. This had been the point of the whole enterprise – to help make the book of Romans accessible to women. But what would the name be?

During the 1st century, when Jesus walked the earth, a Jewish rabbi would have been surrounded by his students, with some of the men sitting as his feet to learn and listen. This was the custom, the understood norm of the day. But in Luke 10:39, Mary sat at the feet of Jesus. Mary, a woman, was taught by this unconventional rabbi. Mary was given the dignity of taking in his words, his pauses, his tone. She was as worthy of his teaching to Jesus as the men in the room, as are we, his women students today. And so we are At His Feet Bible Studies, hoping to sit at the feet of Jesus while we study his word.

Please find our other available studies at our website:
www.athisfeetonline.com

Acknowledgments

Hope: I have to thank all the people in my world who are always cheering me on. Dr. Ray-Ray, who equal parts makes me laugh and challenges me in all the places I get stuck, you are the best husband I could ask for. To my children, Cana, Thea, and Nias, who are so proud that their mom "has a book," I love you on good days and bad. To my parents, who always have my back with love and words of belief in me. TCU Sisters, you are the ultimate hand holders who always cheer me on and love me every step of the way. To Joy and Natalie, your faith in me always surprises me and gives me courage when I need it most! And to Renae, the best editor a girl could ask for, who "polishes" us up while always telling us this is good stuff and worthy to be written.

Chris: To my coffee fairy, you know who you are. You have literally made my thoughts more clear on many a day, and I am so thankful for your tangible help. To Michael, who, whether he likes it or not, has become my first line of defense for all theological questions; you are still my favorite human. To Rebecca Brown, you have met me in the darkest places and not been ashamed of me. You help me keep going. RT and Jen, your voices on my Vox are often a lifeline. To the S- moms, thank you for being my constant encouragement and for making me laugh. Mollie, I still can't believe I get to live in the same town with you. You are such a safe place. Ally, you've opened our eyes to a whole new world of how God loves us, and that knowledge has made its way into my writing. And Renae, you work magic, practical magic.

Contents

Study 1

Servants of Christ Jesus

Read Acts 16

In order to get an overview of the historical context for the book of Philippians, please read Acts 16. If you have a little more time, try to read through the whole book of Philippians as well. Otherwise, just skip down to the background summary below.

Background Summary

As is often the case, God began the church at Philippi using unexpected means—closed doors and a stint in prison. Twice in Acts 16, we are told that the Holy Spirit did not allow Paul and Timothy to go through with their plans to preach the gospel in Asia. They must have asked, waited, found one closed door to Asia, asked, waited, and been turned away again in Bithynia. These two men were traveling around the ancient world "strengthening the churches" with Silas (Acts 15:41), telling believers about decisions that had been made by the apostles and elders in Jerusalem regarding holy living for Gentiles. Remember that at this point the church, as a whole, was only about fifteen to twenty years old. The mission to the Gentiles was young, and patterns of Christian living were not yet well established for all cultures.

Finally the Lord opened a door, speaking to Paul in the night with the vision of a man in Macedonia asking for help. Paul and his companions obeyed, taking a boat through the Aegean Sea, reaching land in Neapolis, and finally ending up in Philippi, about ten miles inland. The closed doors in Asia led these missionaries to the Philippians, where God had already been at work.

Named for Philip II, king of Macedonia in 356 B.C., Philippi in the first century B.C. was partially populated by Roman war veterans. They'd been given land that was stolen from native Philippians by Augustus, later to be Rome's first emperor. Philippi was on the Via Egnatia, which at the time was THE major road of the Roman Empire, making it an important trade city. As a Roman colony, Philippi theoretically had the same rights as any city on Italian soil. However, Philippians paid no taxes and were allowed to govern themselves. The city Paul walked into during his first visit in 49 A.D. would have been a busy political center, populated by somewhere between ten and fifteen thousand Greeks and Romans.

God had been working ahead of Paul and his friends in the hearts of a group of women in Philippi, drawing them to the God of Israel. When Paul and his companions arrived in the town, they did not find a synagogue, which required ten Jewish men. However, when they went to the river on the Sabbath, where they assumed they might find a place of prayer, they found both Jewish women and Greek women who were already practicing some of the Jewish religion. Among these women was Lydia, probably a wealthy merchant, who was soon converted and baptized. She opened her home to Paul and the others, and it served as a focal point for the growth of the church in the city.

While in Philippi, Paul exorcised a demon from a slave girl and angered her owners by cutting off their source of income from her fortune telling powers. This landed him and Silas in jail after a heavy beating, which must have greatly discouraged and even confused the baby church at Philippi. But when God sent an earthquake and opened the doors and prisoners' bonds, the jailer who was in charge of them was converted. This led to the jailer and his entire household being baptized, resulting in growth for this little Philippian church.

Fast forward ten years. Apparently, the Philippians, though not a wealthy church as a whole, have sent several financial gifts to Paul since his visit. They have probably also sent multiple letters. He writes them now having had a relationship of mutual ministry and encouragement for years. He is probably under house arrest in Rome awaiting trial. The Philippians know this and are concerned for him. They send Epaphroditus with yet another gift, to encourage Paul, but Epaphroditus becomes ill. Paul sends Epaphroditus back to relieve their anxiety and to pass a letter to them. He plans to send Timothy and then hopes to visit himself.

So what does Paul need this beloved church to know? What precious subject does he broach in a letter to be delivered by hand, requiring days of dangerous and expensive travel? Paul writes to restore Epaphroditus and to thank the Philippians for their gift. He also writes to reframe for them his imprisonment. He has suffered, for sure, as they would have remembered Paul's time in prison while in their own city. But Paul wants to encourage them by telling them the good that has happened because of his chains. He wants them, and subsequently us, to use him as an example of how to live as believers while suffering through hardships, persecutions, and trials. From his place of chains, Paul writes over and over about joy.

But Paul writes for another reason: to confront their disunity. Paul names two women specifically whom he respects as coworkers and who struggle to "agree" or just get along. Notice that Paul does not write these women off or dismiss them. He confronts them head on as fellow ambassadors for Christ. They matter. Their actions matter. Their attitudes matter.

A little historical context is helpful here. According to Gordon Fee, "there is good evidence that in Greek Macedonia women had long had a much more significant role in public life than in most other areas in Greco-Roman antiquity" (26). Three of the names mentioned in the Philippian church are women. Put these facts together and you have a young church full of independent, strong women who were used to being in charge. Is it a wonder that Paul's love for them in a letter includes a directive toward humility?

Paul's words, directives, and encouragement are just as pertinent to twenty-first-century women as they were to those in the first century. May we hear what the Spirit says to his church, and may God grant us the will to be, as Paul writes in chapter 2, "of the same mind, having the same love, being in full accord and of one mind."

Read Philippians 1:1–2

Observation Questions

1. What do you already know about the book of Philippians prior to this study?

2. What do you hope to gain by studying Philippians?

3. If you read the entire book once through, what themes did you notice?

Verse 1. Letters in Paul's day almost always followed a particular form: sender, receiver, greetings, and a wish for good health. Here we see Paul employing the same form but in a distinctively transformed way. First, the senders. Paul is writing along with his co-sender, Timothy, the son of a believing Jewish mother and a Greek father whom Paul had circumcised for the purpose of evangelism among Jews. Timothy was probably the one physically writing the letter as Paul dictated. What was Paul's title for himself and Timothy? Leaders of the great church? Executive directors of evangelism? No. Servants of Jesus Christ. The word "servants" here is better translated "slaves," a term that would have been familiar to first-century people, as many were held as those "subservient to the master of a household" (Fee, 63). Paul believed himself to be personal property of Jesus Christ, the master of his household. And so he chose this as his title. If Paul had had an office, the nameplate on the door would have read, "Slave of Jesus."

Next, the recipients. Notice that Paul does not address "the Philippian church" or "my Christian friends at Philippi" or even "my brothers and sisters at Philippi." He addresses them as the saints in Christ Jesus. This is their distinguishing attribute, their distinctive classification. Before all else, they were saints in Christ. But unlike our twenty-first-century interpretations of the word *saint*, which include things like exceptional holiness of life or virtue, Paul would have meant for these people to understand themselves as the Old Testament people of God were designated: holy ones. This is not holy in the sense of extraordinary or amazingly virtuous but holy meaning "set apart, used for something else." As Karl Barth writes, "Holy people are unholy people who nevertheless as such have been singled out, claimed, and requisitioned by God for his control, for his use for himself who is holy" (qtd. in Garland, 189).

in Christ Jesus. This phrase speaks to the Philippians' union with Christ, their unbreakable connection with him. Paul essentially addresses these dear brothers and sisters by saying, "To you, the men and women who have been chosen and claimed by God for his holy work, who are unshakably connected to Jesus." Is this the way you define yourself? Is this your first thought when someone asks who you are? Unlike the voices in our heads who accuse, God names us first this way, as the ones he picked and tethered to Jesus.

Verse 2. Finally, greetings and a wish for good health are sent as Paul speaks grace and peace to the Philippians. This is how God approaches his chosen people, with grace and peace. As Fee writes, "The sum total of God's activity toward his human creatures is found in the word 'grace.'. . . Nothing is deserved, nothing can be achieved" (70).

Reflection Questions

4. After the Holy Spirit twice prevented Paul from entering Asia, he had a vision of a man asking for help, which led him to go to Philippi. What are your thoughts on the Holy Spirit preventing Paul from going to one place in order to lead him to another?

5. Paul's time in jail, in and out of Philippi, greatly shapes how he encourages the Philippians. Who in your life has used their suffering to encourage you?

6. What was going on with women in the church that prompted Paul's letter? How have you experienced this in your church?

7. Paul refers to himself and Timothy as "servants of Christ Jesus," which essentially means "slave of Jesus." How would seeing yourself as the property of Jesus change your current outlook?

8. Paul's greeting extends grace and peace, or unmerited favor and freedom from disturbance, through God our Father and the Lord Jesus Christ. Which of those two things is your heart longing most for right now?

Focus verse: *Grace to you and peace from God our Father and the Lord Jesus Christ.*
Philippians 1:2

Reflections, curiosities, frustrations:

Study 2

Bring It to Completion

Read Philippians 1:3-11

Observation Questions

1. What is Paul thanking the Philippians for?

2. Why does Paul feel so strongly about them?

3. What is Paul's prayer for them?

Verses 3-6. Right away Paul describes his experience of praying for the Philippians as one of joy. Why? It can't be because of his circumstances—he's imprisoned. In fact, Christian joy has nothing to do with our situation. The joy of the believer transcends all difficulties and discomforts because its source is not our circumstance. It is rooted in the promise that Jesus is the same yesterday, today, and forever. It originates in the confidence that all of Jesus's promises of presence and relationship are trustworthy.

Paul uses the word "partnership" in verse 5 the way we would talk about a trade union or some other group that exists for the benefit of its members. He considers the church in Philippi his collaborators, his teammates. And the fruit of transformed lives that he has seen in them over the past ten years makes him confident that it has been God working in them. God has worked salvation in them and will continue to sanctify them until the day of Christ Jesus, the second coming of Jesus. Our hope for sanctification is the same today. God wooed us, began the work of his Spirit within us, and has committed himself to completing our transformation until Jesus himself returns for his children. We needn't be discouraged when we see clearly our own sin, our slow growth, our clumsy faith. The Lord is the author, the beginner, the creator of our faith. He is also the sustainer and the finisher. He does not press pause on our sanctification because we've been lazy or bad, too angry or forgetful. He does not roll his eyes in disgust when we pass another day without reading our Bible. He draws us to himself, using whatever means necessary, seeing, loving, and knowing us all the while, moving us closer and closer to perfect union with him.

Verses 7-8. Paul continues his declaration of the accuracy of his opinion of these saints, as they have supported him whether he was doing active ministry or suffering in prison because of it. These brothers and sisters are not sending money based on the number of conversions or new cell groups. They are committed to Paul and to the spread of the gospel, because the Spirit lives in them.

Verses 9–11. As the church continues to pray for Paul, he continues to pray for them. Specifically, he prays that their love would grow in certain qualities. We learn from this passage that Christian love is not rash, careless, or automatic. It discerns and tests, evaluates and thinks. Paul is asking this, as Gordon Fee writes, "so that the faculty for making proper assessments about what is absolutely essential regarding life in Christ will increase as well. For truly Christian life, some things matter, and others do not" (101).

Remember that the Philippian church struggles with unity. Surely Paul's specific prayer is targeting their disunity, one of Satan's favorite playgrounds in the church. In Galatians 5:6 Paul writes, "For in Christ Jesus neither circumcision nor uncircumcision counts for anything, but only faith working through love." It's like he's saying, "Hey guys, you know that thing you keep arguing about and then talking about each other because of it? And saying how wrong she was or he was when they said x, y, or z? It doesn't even matter. It doesn't even count. You know what does? Faith expressing itself through love. I'm praying that your love grows in such a way that you figure out what counts."

As we see in verses 10 and 11, the goal of this love is purity, blamelessness, multiplied through the hope of Jesus's return. The image is that of a woman or man walking firmly, not stumbling and falling this way and that, not blown around by useless arguments or heated, emotional discussions that don't matter. This woman moves steadily, even if slowly, down the straight and narrow road of righteousness, giving God glory as she does.

Reflection Questions

4. Paul is praying in joy for the Philippians while he's imprisoned. How is this possible? What limits you personally from experiencing joy?

5. Verse 6 says God has started and will complete a good work in you. What ideas in this verse do you struggle with? What part gives you hope and comfort?

6. Part of Paul's prayer is for the church to have knowledge (facts, information, skills) and discernment (ability to perceive or judge well) in large amounts (verse 9). What are you currently longing for knowledge and discernment about?

7. Paul's prayer is all to prepare for and will culminate in the "day of Jesus Christ." How would meditating on Christ's return change how you view this week's plans?

8. Is there a current topic or area you are struggling to find unity about in your current church? In what ways has this passage reoriented your heart on this?

Focus verse: *And I am sure of this, that he who began a good work in you will bring it to completion at the day of Jesus Christ.*
Philippians 1:6

Reflections, curiosities, frustrations:

Study 3

Christ Is Proclaimed

Read Philippians 1:12-18

Observation Questions

1. What has been made known to the imperial guard?

2. What has Paul's imprisonment done for some brothers?

3. What are the two ways people are preaching Christ?

Verses 12–14. The church at Philippi would have been praying regularly for their friend and mentor, Paul. They received word that rather than growing the church and discipling people as they'd hoped, he'd been captured and put into prison. What? All of this prayer and money and hope for new believers and new churches down the drain! They gathered more money and sent one of their own, Epaphroditus, to comfort Paul. They probably expected him to be discouraged--stuck in jail, in need of food and clothing, his mission on pause.

But no! The "really" in verse 12 is a colloquial term that could also be translated "rather" (Fee, 110-11). So, unlike what the Philippians were expecting, God was using this hard thing for good. It's not that God was not answering their prayers. Instead, he was answering them in a way they had not and could not have anticipated.

The Roman guard was probably not the target audience Paul was expecting. But they were the group of people God had chosen for Paul and his message. The guards, who were probably of the same group of military force whose job it was to protect the emperor and his family, all knew Paul was there because of Jesus. They probably worked in four-hour shifts, meaning at least twelve men were a regular captive audience of Paul. But there were probably others, as David Garland states, "those with legal expertise who were working on the case or the Jewish lobby who brought the charges against Paul" (199).

Here was a group of influential people who had the ear of the emperor rubbing shoulders with Paul. Those in the church at Rome saw that God had put the master evangelist into an interesting place of influence. This strengthened their faith, giving them courage in the Lord to speak about him despite the danger. In a time when Nero was becoming more dangerous, and the threat of punishment more likely, God used Paul's prison term to embolden the Roman church. This is our God—unpredictable, unfettered, free. He is not bound by our plans or expectations. He is not limited by the confines of our imagination.

Verses 15–18. But there was not a universal response of support for and solidarity with Paul. He was probably in prison either because Christianity was not an approved religion in Rome as Judaism had been or because officials were unsure as to whether followers of this religion could call Christ "Lord" in a place where they were politically required to call Caesar "Lord."

These people working against Paul were believers. Paul may have even known some of them. They may have been embarrassed by his chains or envious of his ministry. Whatever the reason, here were brothers, supposed allies in the same city, the same church, trying to inflict pain and more suffering on Paul. We would expect him to feel betrayed, angry, bitter. And he probably was hurt; Paul was human, after all. As Moisés Silva writes, "We would go too far if we imagined Paul gritting his teeth as he speaks of rejoicing, but we may be sure that his joyful response was not natural and easy; it would have been unexpected in view of his trials, and therefore required explanation" (69).

Paul was not some superhuman who was immune to feeling rejected by others or feeling lonely, disappointed, or confused. His rejoicing is not some autopilot reaction no matter what he encounters. Rather, Paul is making a choice, born from years of suffering, made possible by kingdom priorities. Paul's greatest aim is the spread of the gospel; everything else is secondary. As Garland writes, "His private concerns must not outweigh his ultimate task" (200). This flies in the face of our twenty-first-century individualistic paradigm of happiness. It is offensive and foolish, in most of our opinions, to endure harm or pain for the greater good. But Paul has been in Christ's school of suffering for years. He has learned to choose the kingdom and its joy instead of reacting to the roller coaster of circumstances. In fact, as we will see, Paul trusts that even his suffering will, in the end, be used for his good.

Reflection Questions

4. The Lord used Paul's imprisonment, a very difficult situation, to spread the gospel throughout the imperial guard, a wonderful result. When has God used a difficult situation in your life for a surprisingly good result?

5. "This is our God--unpredictable, unfettered, free. He is not bound by our plans or expectations. He is not limited by the confines of our imagination." How have you found this to be true in your life?

6. In verses 15–18, we learn Paul is getting opposition, for unknown reasons, from his own brothers and sisters in Christ. Describe when you have felt such opposition with fellow believers.

7. In reference to your answer to question 6, what were the emotions that arose from that experience? What did you do about it?

8. In verse 18, Paul ultimately celebrates Christ being proclaimed, no matter the motive. Is this surprising to you? Why or why not?

Focus verse: *What then? Only that in every way, whether in pretense or in truth, Christ is proclaimed, and in that I rejoice.*
Philippians 1:18

Reflections, curiosities, frustrations:

Study 4

Suffer for His Sake

Read Philippians 1:18b–30

Observation Questions

1. What is Paul hoping for in verse 20?

2. What are the two options Paul is weighing against each other?

3. According to verses 27–28, what does Paul want to be true of the Philippians?

4. Paul says the church will do what for the sake of Christ?

Verses 18-20. Here Paul tells us the secret behind his confident hope of deliverance and joy. It's not working harder, having the right connections, careful planning, or making sure he keeps everyone around him happy. Paul is relying on two things: the prayers of the church and the Holy Spirit. These are his strategy.

Execution is a real possibility for Paul at this point. He has the audacity to expect that he will be able to honor Christ, or magnify him publicly, whether he lives or dies. Where can we find the confidence of Paul? How can we know that no matter our circumstances, we will boldly magnify Jesus as we grow in our faith? Only through the prayers of his people and the Holy Spirit working through us. This whole notion forcefully opposes our twenty-first-century individualism. Contrary to what is often praised in our culture, we were made to live as DE-pendent people —dependent on God and on others. As Moisés Silva writes, "It is indeed a sobering thought that our spiritual relationship with God is not a purely individualistic concern; we are dependent on the Spirit's power in answer to the intercessory prayers of God's people" (72). This means that our sanctification is not a just-me-and-Jesus enterprise. It is a me-within-the-church-of-Jesus endeavor.

Verses 21-26. Here again we see Paul putting aside his own preferences for those of the kingdom. Remember that he is writing to a divided church. As an example, he uses his own hypothetical choice (though he doesn't really have a choice) of life or death. Clearly death is his inclination. But he gives these divided, probably frustrated and angry men and women an example to follow. He willingly puts aside his own desire. He tells them that for their sake, and in hopes of making another trip to Philippi to pastor them further, he would choose life, even life in prison.

Verse 21 is a litmus test for our own hearts. Is life for us a matter of honoring Jesus (see verse 20), literally enlarging or magnifying him? Or is he a comfortable add-on we turn to when needed? If he were to end our lives today and call us to full and immediate communion with him, would we consider it progress? Do we anticipate it being preferable to the lives we are living now? Idolatry steals away the freedom of joyfully answering yes to these questions.

Verses 27–30. In verse 27, the first verb which is translated either as "conduct yourselves" or "let your manner be" has the feeling of tenacity, and literally it means to "live as citizens" (Fee, 162). But here Paul adds the word "worthy." Citizenship in Philippi was a big deal in Paul's day. In fact, a Philippian citizen technically enjoyed all the rights and privileges of a Roman citizen, a coveted position in the ancient world. These rights would have included voting, standing for public office, and immunity from some taxes. Paul is reminding these believers that just as they are citizens of Rome with its responsibilities and privileges, so too they are citizens of heaven. Their lives should reflect this fact.

Paul intends to send the letter on ahead and then come himself. But before he gets to them, he wants to hear that the Philippians are contending together, working as one body. Their unity and refusal to shrink back from their enemies and opposition would be proof, says Paul, of their enemies' ultimate judgment by Christ and the church's ultimate salvation. Apparently, the Christians were being punished for their allegiance to the Lord Jesus instead of the Lord emperor. Paul was probably in prison for the same reason. Roman citizens would have somehow honored the current emperor at public events. It's very possible that their refusal to show reverence in the prescribed way was causing them serious trouble, and could have maybe even led to prison.

Paul does not tell these brothers and sisters just to hope the struggle goes away, or to pray that God finally hears and makes it stop. On the contrary, Paul tells them that living as people who will only name Jesus as their Lord in a time and place where their culture is punishing them for doing so is a special privilege, a gift from God. What? How? Why? Because for the Christian, the path to splendor must first always go through death. Because the way of the disciple is the way of the master. As Silva writes, "Suffering is the way to glory, God's gift of salvation for his children" (83).

Paul is speaking specifically here of suffering for Christ and claiming our allegiance to him as Lord. For the Philippians, and for us, "suffering is not a sign of their abandonment by God but a sign of special grace granted to them" (Garland, 211). We in the Western church do not yet experience the suffering that our brothers and sisters do in other parts of the world. But the little that we may suffer here and there because of our allegiance to Christ must be counted as an exceptional advantage or benefit, not a punishment. Consider some of the "rock stars" of the faith, if you will. Peter was crucified upside down. Paul was beaten, imprisoned, poor, and misunderstood. Stephen was stoned to death. These are the privileged, the exceptional, the honored. What does this tell you about the life to which Jesus is calling you?

Reflection Questions

5. Paul is dependent on the prayers of other believers and the Holy Spirit to give him joy and sustain him through all things. Do you recognize your dependence on these things? Why or why not?

6. Paul is putting aside his preference of dying and being with Christ in order to remain on earth to be helpful to the church. Where are you currently putting aside your preferences or desires in order to do something greater that the Lord has called you to?

7. When have you ever suffered for the sake of Christ? Did you consider it a gift or a burden?

8. What about the concept of suffering for Christ feels intimidating and overwhelming to you?

Focus verse: *For it has been granted to you that for the sake of Christ you should not only believe in him but also suffer for his sake.*
Philippians 1:29

Reflections, curiosities, frustrations:

Study 5

The Interests of Others

Read Philippians 2:1-4

Observation Questions

1. What are the four things Paul lists that should motivate action for the church in Philippi?

2. How is unity described in verse 2?

3. What two things does Paul say in verse 3 should not be motivation for our treatment of others in the church?

4. Whose interests are we to look after?

As we begin a new chapter, it's important to remember that this is a letter, meant to be read all at once in one sitting. Therefore, we must begin reading chapter 2 with the context of chapter 1 squarely in our minds. Though much of these first four verses could be applied to our lives as Christians in general, Paul wrote these instructions and commands to a divided church as an antidote to the fighting he had heard about.

Verse 1. It is easy to read the "you" in this verse as the second-person singular, leading to a me-and-Jesus, individualized perspective. But Paul intends for the entire sentence to speak to the church as a whole. He is addressing the Philippian church as a body, not as individual believers. When he writes of encouragement, comfort, fellowship, and tenderness, he means that which they have received *from* God *through* one another. Sanctification (growing in Christ) and glorification (final, total unity with him) are corporate endeavors. We are saved into the body, we grow as a body, and we will one day gather around the throne of Jesus to worship as a body.

Verse 2. Paul's "if" in verse 1 is better translated "since." *Since* you've experienced all of these things within the church, you must do what I am asking. And what does he ask of them in response? To be unified in all things, which will fill him with joy. The word translated "complete" is used in Romans and Timothy to mean "to fill someone up with something." Paul tells the church to fill him up with joy by being unified in "mind, heart, and soul" (Chapman, 104). He calls them, in this place of division, to be of "one mind, fellow souled, and loving the same thing" (ibid., 106). What do these words look like lived out, with skin on? The next fifteen verses describe exactly that.

Verse 3. Paul puts together two words to construct what we read in English as "vain conceit." *Kenos* (empty) + *doxa* (glory) = empty glory. This is the craving of reputation and greatness. It is the "race to honors and precedence [that is] threatening community life" (Garland, 214). These Christians were living in a culture that breathed competition and rewarded public status. Everything from your family history, hometown, wealth, and intelligence to your speaking ability was carefully added together to determine your status or worth. This hunger for prestige and position had crept into the church at Philippi and was destroying the body. Most of us could unfortunately describe our own experiences of this in the church, whether brought about by our own vanity and selfishness or by that of another.

But here Paul is calling them, and subsequently us, to be fundamentally different. Instead of valuing their own status or reputation, they needed to pursue humility. At the time, this was something reserved for slaves, for "the insignificant, weak and poor" (Garland, 215). But the character of the kingdom of God is not the same as that of first-century Philippi, first-century Rome, or twenty-first-century United States. In the kingdom, we put others first. We consider them better, not in our assessment of them, but in our consideration of their needs and rights.

Verse 4. We should attempt to care for all of the "interests"— better translated "things"—of our brothers and sisters. Yes, Paul's command is that broad and general. Yes, Jesus told us, you are your brother's keeper.

Paul is not commanding them, or us, to be doormats or to neglect self-care. He is warning against self-centeredness. The church at Philippi was a product, at least partially, of its culture, where phrases like "look after your own things" and "do good to yourself" were everywhere (Garland, 215). Our culture is not so different. "Treat yourself" and "you deserve it" are mantras of the current Western world. We, as daughters of the king, are called to something else.

Reflection Questions

5. How has your experience of encouragement, love, fellowship, and sympathy from Christ and the Holy Spirit affected your treatment of fellow Christians?

6. What does unity in the church look like? What makes you resist unity with your brothers and sisters?

7. Where in your life is your pursuit of empty glory causing tensions and problems in your relationships within the church?

8. What does it look like to live other-centered lives considering others' needs and rights? What is the hardest part of that for you?

Focus verse: *Complete my joy by being of the same mind, having the same love, being in full accord and of one mind.*
Philippians 2:2

Reflections, curiosities, frustrations:

Study 6

He Humbled Himself

Read Philippians 2:5-11

Observation Questions

1. What "mind among yourselves" is Paul wanting for the Philippians?

2. What was Christ's mindset about equality with God?

3. What did Jesus do in human form?

4. What has God given to Jesus as a result of his humility?

Verses 5–8. Though scholars still debate whether these verses were a hymn that existed in the early church before Paul, he makes his theology clear here. Jesus, our elder brother, is a self-sacrificing lover of people who willingly puts privilege aside to liberate those he loves.

But first, where did Jesus begin? As the sovereign, the ruler, God himself. He had every advantage in existence. He gave orders to the morning, showed the dawn its place, and said to the sea, "Thus far shall you come, and no farther" (Job 38:11). There is no power or authority available that he did not already possess. Therefore, no one could ever coerce him into giving anything away. Whatever he did, he did willingly, as the one who rules. Instead of protecting his privileges, he chose to lay them down, set them aside. He stepped down, condescended, relinquished his power.

He made himself nothing. Literally, he emptied himself. This was not a change in his essential nature. His "God-ness" did not and could not be changed. Rather, this was a change in his role, a voluntary shift in his status. Notice the pattern: down, down, down. Down from the ultimate status of almighty to that of a man. Down from omnipotence and blinding glory to the limitations of a human body—hunger, fatigue, disease. He was born in the likeness of men, fully human but "not entangled in our sinful nature" (Chapman, 131). And his condescension didn't stop at the incarnation. As a human, he chose the place of a servant, a *doulos*. In first-century Middle Eastern culture, a *doulos* was "one who [was] devoid of even basic human rights and [was] subject to the will of others" (Garland, 220). Jesus submitted himself to a mother's authority, Roman laws, temple rules. He became obedient, voluntarily limiting the exercise of his rightful authority, to the point of being forsaken, tortured, killed. Down, down, down.

He did not die in an honorable way, the way of a soldier or a good citizen dying for his cause. There was no dignity in his death nor celebration of his life. Crucifixion was reserved for "violent thieves, rebels, slaves" (Chapman, 133). Even in his death he took the lowest place, the position of shame. His death was the opposite of what the Romans would have counted as noble, the opposite of the vain glory against which Paul warns these believers. This is the conduct of the kingdom, the practice of the servant king. "God's power is demonstrated in shame and weakness, which underscores the contrast between the wisdom of the cross and the wisdom of the world" (Garland, 220). Shame and weakness. Dependence, humility, yielding. Voluntary submission. This is the pattern of Christ's dominion. This is what Jesus calls us to, if we claim to belong to him. And so we first must realize what privileges we have been given in this world. In what arenas do we have pull or advantage? Where does our privilege protect us, our status save us? Paul commanded the Philippians to have the mind of Christ, to be willing to put all advantage aside for the sake of their brothers and sisters, specifically in the context of conflict. This is God's call to us, his church, in the midst of conflict and disunity in our lives. In our marriages, our churches, our friendships, our neighborhoods. Christ the King who condescended for our good calls us to do the same.

Verses 9–11. But stopping there is like closing the book after the crucifixion. It's not over! The pattern of the Christian life is always death then life, burial then resurrection, always the kernel of wheat falling to the ground and dying to produce many seeds. Jesus's absolute humiliation was followed by supreme exaltation; there is no higher standing he could attain. There is not a more prestigious name, and a name in Semitic culture means more than just what you call someone. It is their capacity, their job, their basis for existence. Jesus alone now holds this place and this name. Why? Because God put him there in response to his complete self-sacrifice.

Paul makes clear reference in verse 10 to Isaiah 45:22-23, where we read, "Turn to me and be saved, all the ends of the earth! For I am God, and there is no other. By myself I have sworn; from my mouth has gone out in righteousness a word that shall not return: 'To me every knee shall bow, every tongue shall swear allegiance.'" Jesus is being named as the Lord (Yahweh) and God (El), the only God. If they had not yet understood Jesus's equality with the God of the Old Testament Israel up to this point, they can't miss it here. Paul explains that all those now living and those dead ("under the earth") and all angels and all demons will one day bow. He is not predicting a "mass conversion occurring at the end of the age" (Garland, 222). Rather, he explains that all will finally admit Jesus's true identity and authority. Some will do so with joy; others will surely do so on their way to agony. Even those who are currently opposing these brothers and sisters, perhaps making their lives complicated and even dangerous, will bow in deferential respect.

Remember again the context—division, persecution, suffering. This little church needed to hear that at the end of the day, when all of the battles are over and the powers that seem so unmovable on this earth are made to finally come face to face with the Lord, none will be left standing. All will bow to the true king. For us, the message is the same. All who work with us, all who work against us; every friend and every enemy; our teachers, mothers, pastors, friends, and children; all will take the posture of a servant and say the words with their lips that they have been made to say: You are the Lord. There is no other.

And so the kingdom life pattern of death and life, shown so clearly in the life of Jesus, is the pattern of his followers as well. Paul explained this suffering that leads to glory in Romans when he wrote, "if children, then heirs—heirs of God and fellow heirs with Christ, provided we suffer with him in order that we may also be glorified with him. For I consider that the sufferings of this present time are not worth comparing with the glory that is to be revealed to us" (Romans 8:17-18) Oh, Lord, let us see clearly the glory that is coming, that we may consider our present struggle not even worth comparing to that great day.

Reflection Questions

5. What is your reaction to this thought from the commentary: "There is no power or authority available that he did not already possess. Therefore, no one could ever coerce him into giving anything away. Whatever he did, he did willingly, as the one who rules. Instead of protecting his privileges, he chose to lay them down, set them aside"?

6. Jesus was placed in human history with no power, a doulos, someone who had to submit to authority in every area of his life. How does this affect your view of his sacrifice for us? Your view of humility?

7. Paul wants the Philippians to take on this mindset of Christ as they interact within the church. How does this mindset currently affect areas in your heart as you relate to brothers and sisters around you?

8. Paul describes a day when every person and all authority will submit to the name of Christ. What about this is exciting and comforting to you? What part is scary?

Focus verse: *Therefore God has highly exalted him and bestowed on him the name that is above every name, so that at the name of Jesus every knee should bow, in heaven and on earth and under the earth.*
Philippians 2:9–10

Reflections, curiosities, frustrations:

Study 7

It Is God Who Works

Read Philippians 2:12-18

Observation Questions

1. According to verse 13, what is God working in you to accomplish and for what purpose?

2. Define the words *grumbling* and *disputing*.

3. According to verses 15-16, what does Paul hope will be the result of his life's work and ministry?

Verses 12–13. Before we even start discussing this passage, let's make a helpful distinction between Paul's purpose in Romans and/or Galatians and Paul's point here. In verses like Romans 11:6 ("But if it is by grace, it is no longer on the basis of works; otherwise grace would no longer be grace") and Galatians 2:16 ("yet we know that a person is not justified by works of the law but through faith in Jesus Christ, so we also have believed in Christ Jesus, in order to be justified by faith in Christ and not by works of the law, because by works of the law no one will be justified"), Paul is explaining how a person is saved—the *means* by which a person receives salvation. It is by grace through faith. It cannot be earned. Good works cannot buy it; the end. But that's not the point Paul is making in Philippians 2. Here he is writing to believers who understand grace through faith. The means of salvation is not the issue they're struggling with presently. Instead, Paul, the pastor, speaks directly to their present need, exhorting them to follow the example of their master. He tells them to practice humility as a prescription for the division happening in their church. He is showing them how to work out their salvation. These people have received salvation. Paul is telling them what to do with it. As he writes in Ephesians 2:10, "For we are his workmanship, created in Christ Jesus for good works, which God prepared beforehand, that we should walk in them." We are saved for good works, not by good works. The order matters.

Paul knows his friends are suffering, and he encourages them. But the real encouragement comes in verse 13 when he tells them that we work because God works. God is empowering them, energizing them, giving them the will to work. Because God works, they work. And so he can freely say to them, "Work out your salvation. Walk it out. Be obedient." Notice that the attitude we are to have as we do this work is one of fear and trembling, in awe of God and in submission to one another. Here again we see that the "your" in the phrase "work out your salvation" is plural.

This is not an individual salvation but a corporate one. We are saved into a body. As David Garland writes, "the community of Christians is God's laboratory that is designed to work out God's purposes" (225). We, as a body, work out our salvation together. So that girl who drives you crazy with all of her drama? How you respond to her is part of you working out your salvation. The lady who seems to always be telling you she's praying for you? Letting her do so, and telling her what you need prayer for is part of working it out. The child that drives you to your knees over and over? Bringing your anxiety to the Lord is working it out. The pastor that isn't quite as gentle as you'd like? Treating him with gentleness in response is working it out. All of these things are part of walking out what God has already given to us, in all of our weakness and stumbling. We work because God works first.

Verses 14–16. "You sound like the Israelites, grumbling in the wilderness," says Paul. "They were supposed to be a light to the nations; now you should be that light. All of your bickering is affecting your witness." The grumbling Paul describes is that quiet, mouth covered, head turned grumbling at the back of the meeting. It's muttering against our leaders. It's fighting and complaining. These are not the bright and shiny actions of those who "shine as lights in the world." In fact, the way we treat one another matters, and it is noticed by our surrounding culture. Of course, there are always things to complain about in the church; it's full of broken people. Part of faithfulness looks like holding our tongues.

Verses 17–18. Levitical priests would have poured out a wine offering in the sanctuary, according to God's command (Numbers 28:7). Paul is comparing himself to this sacrifice as he suffers as a prisoner sent by the Philippians for the sake of mission. But he is not depressed or hopeless; nor does he want his friends to be so. Instead, he tells them to rejoice. But why? Isn't this the opposite of what we would expect Paul to do, and of what the Philippians should be feeling?

Remember how Paul started this letter. Because of his imprisonment, others are hearing the gospel and the Roman church has been emboldened. Because of these things, he rejoices. The final result for Paul and his beloved Philippian church is already known—glory. He refers to the day of Christ in passing because it's already a guarantee. Their end is never-ending joy. Because of this, he is free to rejoice in the midst of prison and uncertainty. As Gordon Fee writes, "Joy has nothing to do with circumstances, but everything to do with one's place in Christ" (257). Paul is showing his brothers and sisters, and therefore us, the way—the path of joy in the midst of suffering. Our place in Christ is the only thing that can enable us to rejoice while we suffer in this world.

Reflection Questions

4. What is your reaction to this statement: "We are saved for good works, not by good works. The order matters"?

5. How have you seen God use the community of Christians to work out his purposes in your life and in the lives of others?

6. Think about the idea that God is always working in you to accomplish his will and good pleasure for the body as a whole. How does this change your view of your current areas of service in the church, whether big or small?

7. Where are you currently having a hard time not grumbling or disputing with your fellow brother or sister in Christ? What are the possible implications of that for those around you inside and outside the church?

8. The call on Paul's life was so hard that he could not rely on circumstances as his main source of joy. Instead, he drew joy from his place in Christ. What are some practical ways you can look past your life circumstances to draw from this steady, unshakable joy?

Focus verse: *For it is God who works in you, both to will and work for his good pleasure.*
Philippians 2:13

Reflections, curiosities, frustrations:

Study 8

Fellow Workers

Read Philippians 2:19-30

Observation Questions

1. How does Paul describe Timothy in verses 19-23?

2. How does Paul describe Epaphroditus in verses 25-30?

3. What appears to be Paul's goal in hoping to send these two men to the Philippians?

Verses 19-21. It may seem upon a first reading of this passage that we've gone from inspiring metaphors of holiness and sacrifice to mundane travel plans. But don't miss what Paul is doing here. In making plans to send Timothy and Epaphroditus, he is doing exactly what he has required of the Philippians—putting others' needs above his own. This is what working out his salvation looks like for Paul. This is what it is to "look not only to your own interests but also to the interests of others." Paul is the one under house arrest, awaiting news of his own trial. Yet his intention is to send his two partners back to the Philippian church. Yes, sending Timothy is partially for Paul's encouragement, to hear about the church's growth and faithfulness. But these two men are examples of the humility described in 2:5-11. In the midst of persecution and suffering, Paul wants to send living examples of his prescription for their disunity.

Paul describes Timothy as being "like-souled" (Chapman, 172). He contrasts Timothy with those in Rome of which he spoke earlier in Philippians 1:17, who preach Christ out of selfish ambition. They are the "all" he refers to here in verse 21. Of course, not every Christian in Rome was insincere. Paul is using hyperbole, a rhetorical tool to call attention to Timothy as one to be emulated.

Verses 22-24. Paul continues to lay out Timothy's credentials. In his day, "one of the best things you could say about the character of any son . . . was that he was attentive to his duties to (and alongside) his father" (Chapman, 175). This is why he says Timothy has proven himself. And so Paul feels confident in his plan to send Timothy in his stead.

Verses 25-28. But before Timothy, Paul will send this letter with Epaphroditus. Don't get lost in the logistics or names here, but follow Paul into these personal, tender moments in the life of the church. Epaphroditus's name was probably some form of the Greek goddess Aphrodite, goddess of love, beauty, pleasure, and procreation. He was probably a converted pagan who had grown to be a faithful and trusted brother in the church. He was sent by the church in Philippi to give Paul food, money, warm clothes, and encouragement. Remember that these were not the eight-hundred- or even three-hundred-member churches of today. This was 60 or 62 A.D. The church worldwide was not yet thirty years old. The church in Philippi was probably only about ten years old, and not very large.

Everyone would have at least known Paul's name, and all would have known Epaphroditus personally. They would have pooled together what they could and sent him out, after much prayer and probably tears, onto a dangerous journey to try to encourage, feed, and clothe their father in the faith. But on the way, Epaphroditus contracted some sort of life-threatening illness, of which there would have been no quick antibiotic at the local urgent care clinic. Their beloved brother almost died. In the Greek, he was "next door neighbor" to death (Garland, 230).

Imagine Paul caring for Epaphroditus on his deathbed, dreading the loss of a trusted friend and co-worker as he awaited what could have been his own death sentence. Think of those in Philippi who had heard rumors of Epaphroditus's illness worrying and praying for him. There was no text, email, or phone that could reassure them of his eventual recovery. Letters were delivered by hand and took weeks to arrive. No wonder Paul wants to send Epaphroditus himself with the letter, commending him as a fellow soldier in the spiritual war of the gospel. Paul knows the church is worried, and he wants them to welcome Epaphroditus as they should, a fellow slave who was willing to die for the sake of others.

Verses 29-30. Notice the appearance of the word "joy" again here. Paul is reframing this brother's homecoming for the church. It could have easily felt like what had happened was a failure—a shortened visit fraught with deathbed sorrow. But Paul directs them again toward joy, because Epaphroditus did for him what the Philippians couldn't do because of their geographical distance.

It is easy to read these words from a cold, distant perspective, like a history textbook full of long-dead, foreign people. But these were real people with friendships, family, habits, favorite foods, sleep problems, bad knees, and close confidants. They missed each other, prayed for each other, and relied on each other. And Paul once again planned to set an example for them by sending his two friends for the good of the church, and at his own loss. He knew what was true then and is still true today: we need examples to follow, people to imitate. We need to see what it looks like to walk out and work out our salvation. We need flesh and blood examples today that look like our ultimate example, who in the most perfect way looked not only to his own interests but also to the interests of others.

Reflection Questions

4. Paul is currently in his own state of need and suffering but decides to serve the church in Philippi by sending these two partners of his to care for them. When have you had someone sacrifice for you even during a difficult time in their own life?

5. Paul had a deep bond with Timothy and describes him as being "like-souled." Where in the church have you experienced a similar level of friendship and like-mindedness? What effect has it had on you and those around you?

6. Epaphroditus had an interesting role of being a go-between for Paul and the Philippian church and delivering in person these precious letters. What do you think that role was like?

7. Again Paul calls the Philippians to joy despite their less than ideal circumstances. What attitude instead of joy would your heart be tempted to have if you were in a similar situation? Why?

8. What is your main takeaway when you read and learn the details of the lives of those in the Bible, such as these details about Timothy, Paul, and Epaphroditus?

Focus verse: *I am the more eager to send him, therefore, that you may rejoice at seeing him again, and that I may be less anxious.*
Philippians 2:28

Reflections, curiosities, frustrations:

Study 9

Surpassing Worth

Read Philippians 3:1-11

Observation Questions

1. In verse 2, whom does Paul tell the Philippians to look out for?

2. According to verses 5 and 6, what things could Paul have confidence in?

3. Paul views worldly accomplishments as loss or rubbish in comparison to what?

Verses 1–3. Paul doesn't use "Finally" to mean he's approaching the end of his letter. It's more like, "as for the other matters we need to talk about." It's a transition from one topic to another. But before he launches into a warning, he reminds the Philippians of the way to walk through their suffering: by rejoicing. This isn't Paul flippantly telling these friends to put a positive spin on a negative emotion. In fact, it's not passive at all. This is an imperative, a command. It's something he wants them to *do* in the midst of trial. To rejoice means to praise, to sing, to name the good things about God. It's the drum he keeps beating because he knows it is what these Christian believers need to help them persevere, to remind themselves of who God is and whose they are. As David Chapman writes, "Joy is a choice. It is a commitment to rejoice in our relationship to Christ and our identity in him" (198).

Now for the warning. Paul warns these dear brothers and sisters about the Judaizers. These Judaizers are Christians, but they believe Gentiles must first obey the Torah (the Old Testament law) and be circumcised, effectively becoming Jews culturally, before they can be real Christians. Paul uses the strongest language to warn the Philippians—"Watch out! These people want you to believe that you must add something to Christ's righteousness. They're dangerous." Though they have not necessarily penetrated Philippi, Paul has encountered these people in various cities, and he anticipates them trying to convince the Gentiles in the church there to be circumcised. He's obviously warned the Philippians about them before, as he says it's no trouble to repeat himself.

So what's so dangerous? Would it have really been so bad to circumcise the Gentile believers? It certainly would have made the Jewish Christians more comfortable, and may have even spared some in the church persecution. The problem is these Christians are telling Gentiles they must do something outwardly to qualify for grace. They must take a step to right themselves before the righteousness of Christ can be enough. This is not the gospel at all.

And so Paul calls them dogs, which is what Jews normally called Gentiles. He says they are evildoers, as instead of teaching others to rest in the righteousness of Jesus, they push them to add some external act to it. He calls them mutilators—literally, "those who cut to pieces," a play on the word *circumcision*—because they have become no better than those who cut on flesh as in a Pagan ritual. They have it all upside down, he tells them. Circumcision pointed to something else, and that something is circumcision of the heart. Both we former Jews and the Gentiles who worship by the Spirit give glory to Jesus. We are the true circumcision. We put our confidence not in a physical act but in Christ.

Verses 4-6. Paul knows his resume means nothing for the kingdom. So in a moment of sarcasm, it is as if he says, "Oh, you wanna play that game? You wanna play the 'who has more reasons to be confident in what they've done externally' game? Let me give you my list. I was circumcised before those people even knew who Jesus was. I'm from the holiest tribe, raised by two Hebrew speaking Jews, a member of the most rigorous sect who actually call themselves 'the separated ones,' trained in both the written and oral law by the best of the best. I was ahead of everyone my age in terms of punishing those who didn't keep the Jewish law, including having Christians killed. And I kept that law to a T, down to the last detail. When it comes to the type of righteousness the Judaizers can offer you, I can play this game better than anyone else can. Bring it."

Verses 7-8. Paul played the comparison game in Jewish external righteousness and won. But when he encountered Christ on the road to Damascus, he saw clearly that all of his credentials and zeal to work for God's acceptance were not actually advantages. Instead of points that helped gain God's affection, they were loss. Everything he thought was moving him into a better status with God was actually working against him. Why? Because these things "had in reality been working to destroy him because they were blinding him to his need for the real righteousness which God required" (Silva, 157). The first step is admitting we have a problem. Only by renouncing the things we think earn us God's favor can we begin to find righteousness in Christ. The things Paul counted as gain were not bad in and of themselves, but using them as the grounds for his status before God was useless. Paul really did suffer loss. He had an amazing reputation and a bright future being honored in the Jewish community. He was the up-and-coming young Pharisee. But compared to knowing Jesus, all of his former advantage he calls rubbish, literally, "human feces." A new perspective came into place for Paul when he met Christ. Knowing Jesus, for Paul, is not an intellectual exercise or mental assent. This knowing is the knowing between a husband and a wife; it is intimate and personal. It has a history. And its glory far surpasses anything he has ever known.

Verses 9–11. Paul recognizes that his righteousness comes only from being in Christ, in union with him, which happens through faith. This rightness, this right standing with God, is given to him, to the Philippians, and therefore to us, by God. Period. "Grace plus anything cancels out grace" (Fee, 320). This is something that God grants, that God does. We cannot reverse it, add to it, or diminish it any more than we can undo Christ's resurrection (Ferguson, 81). This means that when we've ignored God, ignored his word, spoken harshly to our children, been cruel to our husbands, or sinned in various other ways, God's opinion of us does not change. It also means we cannot make him love or accept us any more than he already does when we give more money, hold our tongue, teach Sunday school, or read our Bible. If our standing depends on Jesus's record, which is finished, then God's opinion of us is fixed, reliable, unchanging. Think about that.

Paul knows Christ. But he wants more. He knows that as God uses him in kingdom work and makes him more like Jesus, he uses suffering to do so. Jesus's resurrection came only after his suffering on a cross. His followers should expect the same pattern. Knowing

Jesus intimately means knowing his experience of sacrifice and death to self. Paul longs for even deeper intimacy with Christ, which only comes through a life with the same pattern—rejoicing in our relationship to Christ in the midst of our suffering.

Reflection Questions

4. In verses 1-3, Paul doesn't merely suggest but commands his readers to rejoice, or to praise, to sing, to name the good things about God. Have you ever tried to do these things when you felt no joy? What resulted?

5. Paul is strongly warning the church that believers who suggest something needs to be added to Christ's righteousness are dangerous. How has this been dangerous in your own life?

6. Paul has quite a religious "resume" in which he could rest. What's on your Christian resume?

7. "Grace plus anything cancels out grace." What is your "plus anything"?

8. Our standing with God is secure, stable, and unshakable based on Jesus's behavior and obedience in our place. What is your heart's response to this—fear or a sigh of relief? Why?

Focus verse: *Indeed, I count everything as loss because of the surpassing worth of knowing Christ Jesus my Lord. For his sake I have suffered the loss of all things and count them as rubbish, in order that I may gain Christ.*
Philippians 3:8

Reflections, curiosities, frustrations:

Study 10

We Await a Savior

Read Philippians 3:12-21

Observation Questions

1. Does Paul consider himself already perfect?

2. What way of thinking or mantra does Paul live by in verses 13–15?

3. In verses 18–19, how does Paul describe those who are "enemies of the cross of Christ"?

Verses 12–13. What is the "this" to which Paul refers in verse 12? All of the things he just mentioned in verses 10–11: knowing Christ and the power of his resurrection, sharing in his sufferings, becoming like him in his death. Paul is talking about the already–not yet of this world. The kingdom of God is already in place, but it has not yet come in its fullness, as it will when he returns. Therefore, Christ's work in Paul has not yet reached its completion, when he will be perfect, not in the moral sense, but in the sense of being fully mature. Paul is still a sinner, still struggling with obedience. But as he struggles, he pushes forward in his walk, forcing himself to keep going. Like a runner nearing the finish line of the race, he "extends himself forward—he strains forward to what lies ahead" (Chapman, 225).

Verses 14–15. The image of a race continues. Picture a starting line full of runners. A gun is fired, and in a flurry of breath and movement, they leap off the line, find their pace, set their eyes on the finish line. Those who finish well receive their prize. In our race, the gun that begins the race is the call of God to salvation. The call Paul speaks of here is not to a particular vocation or particular action. It is the summons of Jesus to his children to come to him, to abide in him, to be his. And what is the prize at the end of this race? There are many, including a resurrected body, eternal life, and rewards, but the most precious prize is perfect, unimpeded fellowship with Jesus. All of the wondering about whether he hears, whether he sees, will be over. All of the longing to see him, touch him, really know him and be known fully, will end. All of the struggle to obey, to be like him, to be undistracted by the things of this world, will be finished. We will be with him utterly, permanently.

Verses 16–19. Paul is absolutely sure of this model, this pattern, this way of life for the believer, and he has confidence that those who belong to God will eventually see life in the same way. For now, he urges them, and us, to live up to, or literally, "get in line with" or "be guided by" what we have already attained. And what is that? We have already attained the righteousness of Christ, which, as David Garland says, "excludes all boasting, vanity, and haughtiness toward others" (171).

We should follow the example of Paul in his dependence on Jesus. And not just the example of Paul but also of Timothy and Epaphroditus, who were well known to the Philippians. And not just of them, but of mature Christians all around us. There is a recognizable path, a template of the cruciform life. And there are people around us, as there were for Paul, who walk this path. We are to identify them and imitate them, because in them, as Sinclair Ferguson writes, "the pattern of Christ's own life is reproduced" (90).

What about those who claim to be Christians but don't live out this pattern? Paul speaks heavy words about these people, calling them enemies of the cross. They live no differently than Pagans, claiming the name of Jesus but refusing to live like their master. Instead of being ruled by Christ and his kingdom as their priority, they are ruled by their "stomach" or "flesh." They live a "self-centered, self-indulgent existence controlled by illicit desires" (Garland, 247).

Verses 20–21. Some of the brothers and sisters in Philippi were actually Roman citizens, having all of the rights and privileges of a person living in Rome. They understood themselves as an outpost of another kingdom, with their true citizenship in another place. This is exactly what Paul points to as he says that in the same way, your true citizenship is not on this earth but is in another place. Your genuine home, your legitimate allegiance, your proper resting place is heaven. No wonder we feel so out of place here sometimes! Deep in our souls we know this is not the way things are supposed to be. We long for things to be made right, to be fully satisfied and completely content. This is not just a spiritual longing but also a physical one. And Jesus will transform our "lowly body" to be like his. This is not saying that flesh is bad and spirit is good.

Paul is saying that our current bodies will die because of the curse, but we will follow our elder brother and be given a new, resurrected body, free of pain, disease, and death. How? By the same power that was given to Jesus by the Father: "For by him all things were created, in heaven and on earth, visible and invisible, whether thrones or dominions or rulers or authorities—all things were created through him and for him. And he is before all things, and in him all things hold together" (Colossians 1:16-17). HE is the prize at the end of this race, and he is worth the running.

Reflection Questions

4. Is it comforting to think about Paul still struggling with sin and not having reached perfection in this life? Why or why not?

5. "All of the wondering about whether he hears, whether he sees will be over. All of the longing to see him, touch him, really know him and be known fully will end. All of the struggle to obey, to be like him, to be undistracted by the things of this world will be finished. We will be with him utterly, permanently." Which part of this picture of heaven are you most excited for?

6. Who are the mature Christians currently in your life? What have you learned by watching them?

7. In verse 19, Paul gives this description of those claiming to be Christians but aren't: "Their end is destruction, their god is their belly, and they glory in their shame, with minds set on earthly things." What are some concrete examples of what this looks like?

8. Like the Philippians, we are dual citizens of this world and the kingdom of God. Where in your life do you feel this tension most?

Focus verse: *But our citizenship is in heaven, and from it we await a Savior, the Lord Jesus Christ, who will transform our lowly body to be like his glorious body, by the power that enables him even to subject all things to himself.*
Philippians 3:20–21

Reflections, curiosities, frustrations:

Study 11

Rejoice in the Lord Always

Read Philippians 4:1-9

Observation Questions

1. What does Paul ask of Euodia and Syntyche?

2. What does Paul ask the Philippians to do instead of being anxious?

3. What are the eight things Paul asks them to think on in verse 8?

Verses 1–3. Paul's affection for these, his spiritual children, cannot be contained. Their maturity is his reward. He bridges his previous teaching to his next bold words with this display of tenderness. And then comes the moment of truth, the words for which some commentators think this entire letter was preparing. Paul publicly calls out two prominent women of the church, begging them to agree. He uses the same word he used in 2:2, urging them to be "of the same mind." These two women's serious disagreement could possibly have been the beginning and core of the church's disunity. Paul doesn't mince words. He has spent three chapters explaining the way of self-sacrifice to prepare them to hear him beg for their reconciliation.

Euodia ("Success") and Syntyche ("Lucky") had Pagan names and were probably early Gentile converts. These were not outside, fringey troublemakers. They were pillars of the church, fellow workers with Paul, godly, respected, believing women who had a disagreement. It was probably about some practical outworking of their shared faith. But their clash grew, people took sides, and bitterness and resentment spread. The repercussions of their conflict were large and dangerous. Paul does not shame or dismiss these women. Nor does he discuss particulars. He asks the church to help them, dignifying them with descriptors along the way. Love doesn't skirt around uncomfortable situations. Nor does it blow them out of proportion. It tenderly entreats the body to help. Why? Because, as Sinclair Ferguson writes, "Paul makes clear that division between two individuals in a Christian fellowship can never remain a private matter between them. It inevitably affects others" (99).

Verses 4–6. Here he goes again, telling us to rejoice. This is no spontaneous emotion. Christian joy is something we must practice, like gratitude. It is an attitude, a posture, a point of view. It believes that despite what we see around us, we choose to let what God says be most influential in our lives. Paul is, in effect, telling these believers to meditate on what God has said. The Lord will return, he reminds them. And how foolish will we feel when he finds us fighting about trivial practicalities? Paul knows those in Philippi live under the daily stress of persecution and fear, so he speaks directly to that fear, telling them to replace their anxiety, the root of which means "to be pulled apart," with thankful prayer (Garland, 253).

Verses 7–9. Easier said than done, right? But Paul gives us three encouraging words about this anxiety we all fight. First, he promises God's peace, explaining its presence like a "military garrison" (Ferguson, 104). The Philippians would have understood this, as their town was constantly guarded by an outpost of Roman soldiers, stationed there to shield their town. When we speak to God about all of our concerns with thanksgiving, Paul says God sends his peace to safeguard our hearts and minds.

But Paul gives them a second piece of guidance. He knows that freedom from worry does not come by trying to empty our minds of our concerns. Instead, once we've given our worries to the Lord, we must fill our minds with other things. Paul gives these dear brothers and sisters an entire list of worthy subjects, healthy material for meditation. Implied in this command is the fact that God cares what we think about, and that we have the ability to control it. This is not an easy fix; our minds are sinful and lazy, prone to wandering and idolatry. But our brains can be trained to meditate on things that are true, innocent, honorable, and pleasing to God.

Paul describes the stockpile of thoughts that Christians should have on hand. These thoughts should be

- true—in the shape of the gospel with nothing false in them;
- honorable—completely above reproach, such that others would respect them;
- right—to the Roman, this meant conforming to custom or law; to the Christian, it meant righteous, conforming to God's law;

- pure–probably from the practice of setting something apart to be used in the Pagan temple, but Paul Christianizes it to mean something chaste, untouched by evil or sin;
- lovely—considered lovely by the world, like a Bach cantata or a relief worker rescuing trafficked women;
- admirable—being praised, positive attitudes as opposed to grumbling;
- excellent—morally excellent, contributing to the welfare of society in general;
- praiseworthy—things that God will commend us for.

What are some concrete examples of these? Things like the truth of the Trinity or the beauty of a fall leaf, the giggle of a baby or a fellow saint's life story, a good soup recipe or the sovereignty of God; all of these are worthy of our attention and reflection. Paul concludes this instruction by pointing to himself as an example, not out of arrogance, but because he knows we need skin-on representations of the cruciform life. Paul's third encouragement is the most powerful. In our fight to train our minds against worry, selfishness, and a host of other destructive thought patterns, not only will God give us his peace, but the God of peace himself will be with us in the midst of our struggle.

Reflection Questions

4. So much of this letter is to deal with the effects of a conflict two key women in the church are having. When have you seen a conflict like that in a church you attended? What resulted?

5. Think about this definition of joy and gratitude: "It believes that despite what we see around us, we choose to let what God says be most influential in our lives." What's blocking joy currently for you? What is God saying to you about this circumstance through His Word and Spirit?

6. Philippians defines anxiety as being pulled apart or having a divided mind. Where currently is your mind being pulled apart with worry? Write a prayer of thanksgiving.

7. Paul says that just as the ruling authorities would send in troops to guard their territories, so does God send in his peace to guard our hearts and minds through prayer. As you have prayed, when have you found this to be true?

8. Paul encourages the Philippian believers after they have brought their burdens to the Lord to then fill their mind with worthy things to meditate on. Give an example of one of those eight things he suggests and what that has looked like practically for you.

Focus verse: *Do not be anxious about anything, but in everything by prayer and supplication with thanksgiving let your requests be made known to God. And the peace of God, which surpasses all understanding, will guard your hearts and your minds in Christ Jesus.*
Philippians 4:6–7

Reflections, curiosities, frustrations:

Study 12

Through Him Who Strengthens Me

Read Philippians 4:10-23

Observation Questions

1. What secret has Paul learned?

2. What have the Philippians done for Paul financially?

3. What does Paul ask them to do for the saints?

Verses 9–13. Apparently Paul had not received any gifts from the Philippian church for quite some time. They had sent him money multiple times in the past, and then came a long silence. Paul recognizes that this church hasn't had the opportunity to give, perhaps because they haven't had the means. More likely is the possibility that they lost track of Paul as he was moved around the Roman prison system. Remember there were no emails, phone calls, or tracking systems. Word of mouth and hand-delivered letters took time.

In the meantime, God was continuing to teach Paul how to live above his circumstances. Notice that Paul has "learned" to be content. This implies that he, and we, are not born with this ability. Our hearts want more, different, better. We are controlled by our circumstances and surroundings. Contentment seems like a pipe dream—unattainable. But Paul continually uses himself as an example, someone to be imitated. And so, as impossible as it may seem, he shares with us his secret. First, he tells us that learning contentment is not magical or free of pain. It is a process that involves living through the very ups and downs we so want to avoid. Paul lived through humiliation and abundance. He went to bed hungry and knew days of plenty. This ride of the joys and struggles of living in a broken world is familiar to us. What's so new? Here is Paul's secret, and a verse that is so often taken terribly out of context: "I can do all things through him who strengthens me." The "all things" here is not any outlandish endeavor we dream up but is the stuff of verse 12. Paul can be content in any circumstance because of—and only because of—Jesus's power within him. He doesn't do this by looking inward, by amazing self-restraint or self-discipline. The secret he has learned is that of dependence. He leans on, abides in, begs of, delights in, and looks to Jesus. In everything. Not only does he do this when he is in need, in humble, hard circumstances. He does so in abundance, when he is well supplied. The danger of self-sufficiency in times of

70

plenty is just as menacing as the struggle to be content in times of drought. In these two extremes and all of the places in between, Paul points us toward constant dependence on Christ.

Verses 14–18. Any kind of partnership with Paul was potentially dangerous. He acknowledges the Philippians' longtime partnership with him in his mission, calling it in the Greek "fellowshipping with me in my tribulation" (Chapman, 266). It was not just the money that was helpful to Paul but the encouragement it brought. Notice, though, that Paul is more excited about what the gift they sent him meant for them. Paul knew that a fairly poor church pooling together a sum of money and sending it with a brother on an expensive journey didn't just come out of nowhere. It meant rich things were happening in them spiritually. It meant God was growing the kingdom in their hearts. This is what he gets excited about in these last few verses.

In their day, it would have been proper for Paul to repay their gift by sending a gift of his own. Clearly he couldn't do that. Instead, Paul reframes their contribution as a gift given to God by pulling on Old Testament sacrificial imagery (Lev. 1:9). Once the bull had been prepared, cut, washed, and so on, parts of it were burned on the altar of God. The aroma pleased God, not because he had a penchant for steak, but because of the obedience and willingness of the one sacrificing. Paul equates the giving of this little church to that sort of sacrifice. It pleased God and was evidence of fruit in their lives. In the same way, we can please God with our actions. We broken, sinful, selfish people can somehow bring pleasure to the God of the universe with our actions. This is unbelievable.

Verses 19–23. Surely people in the community gave up specific things in order to send money to Paul. Paul assures them that God is aware of this and will indeed give them their daily bread. His words bring to mind Matthew 6, where Jesus speaks about the clothes, food, and drink we all need. Paul assures these dear ones that as they have sought first the kingdom of God and his righteousness, so God will supply their daily needs.

Paul closes his letter with all of the affection that opened it. He adds one last bit of encouragement, letting them know that even the household of Caesar was not safe from being infiltrated with the gospel of Christ. The very seat of power that sought to oppress them was slowly being penetrated by the news that couldn't be contained. From the first paragraph of this letter to the last, Paul has encouraged these Christians, his partners and collaborators, that God is at work. God is at work using our hardships. God is at work giving us examples to imitate. God is at work changing and sanctifying us. Be encouraged and rejoice, dear ones, for the Lord of glory, who willingly left all privilege behind and entered the darkness of suffering for you, is still at work.

Reflection Questions

4. Have you ever had to stop financially supporting a missionary? What was the circumstance?

5. Paul describes a contentment that is obtained by leaning on, abiding in, begging of, delighting in, and looking to Jesus in everything. Is this how you have thought you obtain contentment? How does it differ from your definition?

6. Paul talks about being able to be content both in plenty and in want, meaning neither status guarantees contentment. How do you struggle with contentment when you have plenty? How do you struggle with contentment when you are in want?

7. The Philippians contribution to Paul was evidence of "God growing the kingdom in their hearts." What recent evidence have you seen in your own life of God growing you in the area of sacrifice?

8. Even in their giving, God would take care of them, resupplying them, so to speak. Where are you currently pouring out and concerned you won't get resupplied? Is that a rational fear?

9. What are your takeaways from this study on the book of Philippians?

Focus verse: *I know how to be brought low, and I know how to abound. In any and every circumstance, I have learned the secret of facing plenty and hunger, abundance and need. I can do all things through him who strengthens me.*
Philippians 4:12–13

Reflections, curiosities, frustrations:

Bibliography

Chapman, David. *Philippians: Rejoicing and Thanksgiving*. Focus on the Bible. Scotland, UK: Christian Focus, 2012.

Fee, Gordon D. Paul's *Letter to the Philippians*. Grand Rapids, MI: William B. Eerdmans, 1995.

Ferguson, Sinclair B. *Let's Study Philippians*. Carlisle, PA: The Banner of Truth Trust, 1997.

Garland, David E. "Philippians." In *Ephesians–Philemon*. Vol. 12 of *The Expositor's Bible Commentary*, rev. ed., edited by Tremper Longman III and David E. Garland. Grand Rapids, MI: Zondervan, 2006.

Silva, Moisés. *Philippians*, 2nd ed. Baker Exegetical Commentary on the New Testament. Grand Rapids, MI: Baker Academic, 2005.

Made in the USA
Coppell, TX
12 September 2021